HOW TO FIND YOUR

MOXIE

A Roadmap to Empowerment

With Grit and Grace

Kendra ♥
Reagan ♥
May you always
know your worth.
♡ Lizz

LIZZ

CARTER CLARK

How to Find Your Moxie

A Roadmap to Empowerment with Grit and Grace

Lizz Carter Clark

ISBN: 978-1-7351657-7-6

Joint Venture Publishing

Blue Sky R&D, LLC

Printed in the United States of America

For Luke, Henry, and Jake.

I hope you will never doubt how loved you are or stray from what you know is true. May you always be kind and compassionate, know your worth, and have Moxie as you find ways to make the world a better place.

Moxie- *noun.*

Dictionary.com defines moxie as: *courageous spirit and determination; perseverance.* I have also heard it associated with having grit, strength, toughness, guts, and boldness.

Moxie isn't something we are born with. Moxie appears when we are able to align triumph over tragedy with purpose. *Purpose* is everything. My moxie has shattered the molds I believed I was expected to fit in, and brought me like a phoenix, through the ashes, to soar above chaos and confusion to become a change-maker. Read on to discover how I found my moxie and how you can find yours, too.

CONTENTS

How to Find Your
MOXIE

The road to empowerment and Moxie
requires collaboration over competition.
Let's empower one another with knowledge and encouragement.

This journey starts with me, _____, on _____.
(your beautiful name)   (date)

•·•

I, _____ have found my Moxie. On this date ____
I choose to empower _____ and
(your beautiful friend's name)
ask that they share this book with someone else and pay
it forward also.

•·•

I, _____ have found my Moxie. On this date ____
I choose to empower _____ and
(your beautiful friend's name)
ask that they share this book with someone else and pay
it forward also.

•·•

I, _____ have found my Moxie. On this date ____
I choose to empower _____ and
(your beautiful friend's name)
ask that they share this book with someone else and pay
it forward also.

THE CONTEXT
of my

MOXIE

1

CHILDHOOD

We are so dysfunctional!" Driving home from a photo shoot for a feature in *Family Magazine*, a 12-year-old me threw a royal tantrum in the backseat of the car. I had screamed it at the top of my lungs, knowing it wasn't true but that it was the quickest way to hurt my mother for saying something that I had allowed to cut me to my core. This could have been anything from, "put your seatbelt on," to "talk more softly;" you know, simple things likely to send a preteen in all her splendor reeling off the edge. But for me, it was more than that: reinforcement that I was unworthy. Criticism had always hit me harshly and I rarely felt like I was enough. We were *not* "Family of the Year," and I wanted everyone to know it.

I was often considered rebellious as a child and in defense of my accusers, my first two words were *No* and *Why?* I had a flair for the dramatics and owned it most of the time, but in reality, I was often pushing against things that didn't feel right. I had a strong sense of intuition and an allergy to inauthenticity. I didn't like the pressure that came with praise. I didn't like the inferiority that accompanied criticism. I didn't like rules that seemed hypocritical. This symphony of simultaneous instruments created an environment in which I struggled to exist. Finding words was never my problem, but finding *constructive*, *meaningful* words to express my feelings, insecurities, and fears was such a challenge that I became more comfortable playing a part.

My acting career began long before anyone ever paid me for it. Growing up, I figured out what worked for me and what would bring the attention I sought. People said I was cute, so I owned "cute." They called me talented, so I sang my heart out and danced my little tush off anytime someone was watching. They called me dramatic, so well … I became an actress. I tried my best to be what I thought was expected of me. Attention and approval were like crack cocaine to little me, and I learned to play whatever role was available. But the problem with performing for approval is that expectations were—and are—always changing. To be a Carter was, at times, exhausting. And when approval is the goal, rejection (real or perceived), can be devastating.

Authenticity has always been a core value in my life, even before I was old enough to know it. I needed it; I craved it. Though I have always been capable of playing the part, it has always been vitally important to me that I understand what is real and what is not. Have I mentioned yet that I freaked out after a dance recital when my dad came to hug me because he had shaved off his mustache and I was *convinced* someone else was impersonating him and trying to kidnap our family?

I had a big imagination and big feelings about life that I didn't have the maturity to process- but I also had a wonderful, loving, supportive childhood. In many ways, I had the luxury of completely feeling all of my feelings because I *was* so supported. My childhood was, in fact, pretty idyllic. We had cul de sac baseball games, dance lessons and recitals, even nightly family dinners and yearly vacations. Despite my feelings of being a fraud because our family (like every family) was made up of flawed humans, it was quite the Norman Rockwell experience. That is until my freshman year of high school hit and my world completely fell apart. Only then did I begin collecting the hard experiences that would eventually add up to my moxie.

Our usual routine consisted of my mom picking up my two brothers, Scott (11) and Cason (13) and me, a 15-year-old freshman, from school. If you're doing the math, I attended first grade twice because I was, "so good at it," I got to help the other kids ... or so I was told. On this particular day, as my mom's car rounded the pick-up line, Scott wasn't there. With red, puffy eyes, my mom explained that he had been diagnosed with a rare bone cancer and they would be leaving for Nebraska that afternoon to visit a specialist and determine next steps. This seemed like a logical and proactive plan at the time. But the way my heart remembers it, Scott and my parents drove away that evening and never came back. Of course, that's not what *actually* happened, but that's how it felt to me. One day, I had endless support in a home full of laughter, the next, I felt completely alone in the deafening quiet. Although Cason and I were close, our coping strategies couldn't be more different. When he had strong feelings, he wanted to deal with them alone. When I had strong feelings, well, I wanted to talk it out, cry it out, and sometimes yell it out to feel them all.

We all made sacrifices in our forever-shifted world. Three years later, I got ready for the prom by myself and locked the door behind me, as had become routine with Scott's treatment schedule, with no one to take a picture or be there when I returned to ask about my night.

Not long after that, Scott died. Our wonderful, faith-filled, strong, cohesive "Family of the Year" was shattered into a million tiny pieces. All we had prayed for, hoped for, believed for, and sacrificed had been reduced to a pile of unmet expectations and brokenness that somehow felt like our collective failure.

My parents were immediately deemed heroes, praised for how well they handled everything. They began speaking to groups of parents with sick children and gracing the pages of the newspaper. Our well-maintained image of strength endured, and the four of us kept moving in the direction and manner we felt we were supposed to. We moved to a new house, my dad took a new job, and Cason went from being the middle child to the only child. I went off to college where no one knew me, and no one knew that I was hurting.

Download your Workbook

Pages for Context/ Childhood here.

For a Desktop Experience, go to:

CollegeMoxie.org/how-to-find-your-moxie

THINGS THAT IMPACT
our

MOXIE

2

CONFUSION

O h. My. Gosh. People are *smoking...!"* My first day as a freshman at the University of Southern California was an eye-opener (and clearly during a time when cigarettes were allowed on a college campus). This was the beginning of my fascination with sociology and my exposure to people from vastly different cultures, codes of ethics, and levels of supervision. Of course, I'd seen people smoke before; some of my best friends in high school occasionally smoked, but they had the good sense to hide it from *adults.*

This, however, was a scene of college students slo-mo smoking on the steps of a school building like it was something to be proud of at Rydell High. My midwestern, debutant self didn't know what to do with this. I was intrigued, but not in an *I wanna light up, too!* kind of way. More like, *Wow, you're doing whatever you want and don't care what people think!* kind of way. That was foreign to me. I was conflicted; impressed, but disgusted. Curious, but repulsed. What was my brain supposed to do with what I was witnessing? Respect it? Condemn it?

It took me a long time to understand and appreciate my classmates, though looking back I now realize we had more in common than I would have ever known then (isn't that always the case?). The idea of owning who you are—even if what you stand for isn't ideal and the bar could definitely be higher—and owning it proudly regardless of outside opinions, was fascinating to me. On the other hand, was what I was witnessing truly what I thought it was? Was *perceived* confidence and coolness, *actual* confidence and coolness? There was more to this story that would slowly unfold as I came to know the humans behind the behaviors. Eventually, I would connect with the hurt in their lives in a way that was much stronger than any snap judgment or baseless assumption I had made that first day.

College campuses are filled with lies. Perhaps every community is, but university campuses are bursting at the seams. Some lies are universal and some unique to its own campus culture, but deep within the expensive gates of prestige lives dark, crafty, seething deceit waiting to prey upon the young, optimistic, and searching. We tend to believe these lies because many have been there longer than we have. They're perpetuated by those they serve and those who buy into the belief that in order to fit in, one must embrace the lie. Yet, just because something is shocking doesn't mean it's cutting edge and needs to be celebrated (said no theater department, ever). In contrast, just because a behavior is normalized also doesn't mean it's good or healthy.

Now, after years of working with college-aged women in my adult life, I can spot these lies quickly, simply by asking questions. Students don't typically identify them as easily, but when they talk about the pressures they feel and insecurities they have, the lies are exposed. They show up as: "I have to be *this* size to be pretty."

"I have to party *this* many nights to be relevant."

"I have to get *this* many likes on a social media post or no one cares."

"I have to pull all-nighters this week or I'm not working hard enough."

None of these beliefs are true, nor are they serving anyone. But because of how scary and lonely it can seem to call them out, we choose to buy into them instead of stopping to question and challenge them.

I started the nonprofit, College Moxie, after watching these lies overtake capable, intelligent, beautiful women, year after year. I saw these amazing freshmen come in, excited to boldly take on the world, and it angered me to watch as their confidence was completely drained by sophomore year. They were bitter, jaded, and disappointed, and didn't realize that they had handed their self-worth over to a toxic campus culture or sometimes a group of men who had done absolutely nothing to earn it.

What was happening? Since I saw it consistently in the regions where I served, I decided to see if it was a nationwide epidemic. I held focus groups across the country asking, "What are the biggest issues facing you as a woman on campus today?" Most of the time I didn't have to say anything else. It was all confirmed: women shared fears, disappointments, misconceptions, discomforts, and unmet expectations, but outside of my prompting, *no one was talking about them.* Every woman felt like she was the only one. My heart broke as I discovered this because I used to be her. I felt a deep, burning sense of social responsibility to do something. I had to find a way to give women safe spaces to talk about hard things. And thus, College Moxie was born.

The women I interviewed had a lot to say and just needed to be asked questions to get the ball rolling. During one of our focus groups, two juniors came in together, chatting about anything and everything, and declared that they had been best friends since freshman year. Their closeness was evident by their body language and banter, practically finishing each other's sentences. One woman shared her experience as a freshman saying, "I would go to a party and see people making out with random guys and like, I didn't feel comfortable doing that, but I did it anyway because I thought that's just what you do here."

Her friend turned to her, hearing this for the first time, and said, "Oh my gosh, me too!" Watching them make this discovery together and further bond over it was fascinating. Not only because they were first recognizing this shared experience here with a stranger, but that *best friends* who believed they shared everything weren't actually talking about things that were uncomfortable and big for both of them. Their fears, their insecurities, ways they bought into the lies, they shared them all. This dialogue happened over and over on campuses everywhere, about everything you can imagine: casual sex, normalizing sexual assault, over-consumption and blacking out, body comparisons … and none of it was good. They were uncovering massive lies, yet they all believed they were the only one in it. Everyone felt alone.

The good news is that once we can recognize the lies, we can then start working to expose them, address them, and kick them off campus. Only then will they no longer be our default beliefs. Have you ever heard about that experiment where a guy gets in an elevator and faces the other direction and eventually everyone else turns around, too? Doesn't that sound silly? But it happened. **Why are we just buying into what we see, instead of listening to that still, small voice inside of us that tells us, *Something feels off? I don't feel comfortable. This isn't good for me.* Are we too busy believing the lie that we are alone, and that if we go against the grain we will not be accepted? We think, *Surely, I am the only one who feels this way.* So not only do we *go along* with the lie, we begin to *perpetuate* the lie until our insecurity-driven behavior becomes the catalyst for someone else to fall into the giant black hole we helped dig.** It wasn't that I needed to be more open-minded about smoking. It was simply that I needed to say, "You do you, but that's not for me," and be equally confident in my own decision made by listening to my gut. Who knows how many adults might not be facing lung cancer today had they felt more comfortable being themselves, instead of buying into a prop to make it *appear* they were confident and didn't care what anyone else thought?

In high school, I knew a group of girls who developed eating disorders together because they were so bonded over the collective belief that they were fat (which, by the way, *none* of them were). As if throwing up together in the girl's bathroom between third and fourth period was somehow the game-changing activity that was bringing them closer together? Lies.

How many people are buying into daily behaviors that aren't serving them, simply because it feels better to be part of something than to be alone? If only they realized the power they might have to inspire someone else to say, "You know what, I'm not feeling that either?"

FOMO is a liar, people. And we have to stop letting it make decisions for us. We have intuition for a reason. That still, small voice deep down that knows what's right? Yeah, it was put there in our humanness to protect us from these very things. When I speak about sexual assault and the fight-or-flight response, I share that many of us have a greater fear of rejection than we do of *death itself.* Did you have to read that twice? We would rather cease to exist than risk being ostracized or not fitting in. On paper, it seems silly and ridiculous, right? But no, friends. It is *real.* It is powerful. It is toxic, and it is REAL.

There is so much empowerment in being able to call out the lies we believe—not just for ourselves, but to help expose them for others, too. No one is benefitting from community behaviors that don't build us up. Whether that's believing that we aren't good enough if we don't own the latest trending denim cut, or that we have to bond over the things we *don't* like about our bodies instead of the things we *do*—when we create community around toxic beliefs, we are keeping ourselves and others from thriving.

Being a woman can be hard. Being a woman in college and early adulthood can be *really* hard. It is a big, scary thing to go from being considered a child with rules and legal guardians, to celebrating a birthday that legally defines you as a self-sufficient adult. I was broken in college. I was lost and I was not ready for the responsibilities that came with adulting. I poured myself into leadership because it allowed me to have control when my life felt so helplessly *out* of control. I realized that what *appears* to be is not always what *is,* and sometimes, just as blurred as a Snapchat filter, it isn't anywhere close.

During this time in my life, confusion was front and center. I was grieving but didn't know what that meant or looked like. I went to school at a time when depression and anxiety didn't have names and certainly weren't normalized, so I didn't have the tools to cope with them. I felt attacked and persecuted at times for questioning things, while others were praised for what I considered offensive actions, and I couldn't make sense of it. The complexity of my circumstances far outweighed the maturity of my problem-solving skills and ability to understand. If only my 18-year-old self had known that she wasn't alone, and that others felt these things, too.

Sometimes, it's easier to buy into the lies—even if they seem ridiculous—because when we see others push against them, they don't always win. In fact, there are often consequences for disrupting the norm. Being brave and creating waves requires moxie. Ironically, being brave also *builds* moxie. When we push back against things that don't serve us and don't build us up, we start to break down beliefs that we accepted because "everyone is doing it." When we risk making waves and choose to be brave, we often discover that we are stronger than we knew. We also experience the power of community and see that we are not alone, because someone hears the first voice, and then someone else. As the chain reaction continues, eventually another small, timid voice will say, "I think that, too." Taking the risk allows others to join us and proves to us that our voice matters and has influence.

When we find community in being brave, we also start to see our support networks differently. College was the first time I looked someone in the eye and thought, "This person is totally lying to me." It confused the heck out of me as I thought, "Why would someone do that? Say something they don't mean, or that they *know* they won't do?" It hadn't occurred to me before then that not all the people in our circles are well-intended. This was a harsh lesson I hadn't yet learned but needed to.

When my brother Scott was sick, people flooded us with support. I was a mess and know now that I developed some abandonment issues during that time, but I always knew that people cared. Our community was so strong and supportive, and to this day, my parents still have some of the most amazing, ride-or-die, drive-ten-hours-to-bring-you-dinner-cuz-you're-sick, kind of friends. When we expose lies and start calling them out, we shift our circles of influence, too. **Sometimes confusion is a choice we make because we don't like that what our heart *want*s and what our mind *knows*, aren't aligned.**

It's hard to stand face-to-face with a person's true self if who they really are is disappointing. Sometimes the people we seek approval from most aren't truly invested in us or what's good for us. That can be a gut-punching reality if it turns out to be a close friend, parent, or significant other. But isn't it better to know the truth rather than burying our heads in the sand to save the energy of conflict for another day? Some people in our lives are much more interested in what is good for *them*; and oftentimes those most likely to give, will attract those most likely to take. This realization has helped me to understand the importance of boundaries and the power of a few solid friendships rather than a need for large circles. Calling out lies and prioritizing facts over feelings empowers us to be able to mitigate confusion and conduct check-ups around the health of our communities.

Download your Workbook
Pages for Confusion here.

For a Desktop Experience, go to:
CollegeMoxie.org/how-to-find-your-moxie

3

COMPARISON

O h, it's all fake. Everything can be faked now." Sitting in a formal study room of a sorority house in southern California, my education on body-conforming apps began as the women demonstrated one after the other. "This button squeezes in your stomach," and, "You can define your abs or chin like this," the lesson continued.

I was mesmerized by the simplicity of the process, but also relieved that these women knew what was *actually* happening. My first experience with this level of image altering had been years ago in my modeling days when I saw myself on the cover of a college magazine in a bikini and realized that I had zero freckles. None! They had all been digitally removed, causing me to wonder for the first time ever, "Are my freckles bad? What's wrong with freckles?"

I was happy to see that these women were empowered with the knowledge that expectations of beauty are often unachievable because they are not real. At least, that's what I thought they understood, until one young woman began telling a story about a recent Halloween debacle. She told us how she had been so excited about her costume as a fidget spinner, lighting up as she described every detail. Her enthusiasm was contagious, her joy almost palpable.

She had *planned*; she had completed a full dress rehearsal with costume, hair and makeup, and she was *pumped*. When Halloween arrived, she dressed to perfection, snapped some pics and hopped on social media to post all about it. When she opened the app, she froze and her heart sank. There, another woman was wearing the same adorable costume. Her sadness wasn't because the other girl was also a fidget spinner, but rather from her perspective that the other girl wore it better. She was prettier. She was taller. She was thinner. She was everything superior, according to our friend.

As she relayed the story, this sweet, dynamic, beautiful young woman became visibly deflated. She was so defeated by her inner dialogue that night, that rather than celebrate, she instead put on her pajamas and crawled under the covers, deciding to stay in for the night. The effects of comparison completely stole her joy both in the moment and while reliving it for me. I was heartbroken for her. And it was the most interesting thing: this vibrant, amazing woman who taught me how every photo we see today is enhanced, had allowed comparison to one of those very photos to make her feel completely inadequate.

How did we get to this place where we assume the best about someone else's story and the worst of our own? Do we believe there's only room for some of us, and that if we aren't the very best, then we're not worthy of existing at all? I see this over and over on college campuses. There's naturally an identity adjustment when going from the relative safety of high school, where you may have been valedictorian or captain of the soccer team, to college where everyone's a stranger and equally high achieving. So it makes sense that the bar has been adjusted. My fascination is with the fact that this kind of perceived rejection requires that we first had to decide that confidence comes from being better than others. Is competition really essential to self-love? Is there not room for all of us to succeed? I don't buy it. I think this is one of the biggest lies on the planet that riddles young people with mental health issues, a missing sense of worthiness, and a "need" for micro-identities and material things to prove our worth and status of superiority over others. It is also the greatest setback to a healthy, proactive version of feminism that can truly make positive change in the world for good, starting with us.

Every single one of us is capable of fully walking in our purpose without being a roadblock for anyone else's journey. We can all matter equally, and furthermore, *benefit* from each other's skills, talents, and differences. Sure, some paths might come with more attention or praise, but does that make any one person's contribution to the world greater or less than another's? I say no—no—no freaking way. We all have different gifts, strengths, and areas of passion. Contrary to what we are taught, collaboration is where the power lies.

When I speak about breaking free from comparison culture, I often talk about something I call, "filtered thinking": thoughts that become beliefs that we run our decision-making process through. For many women, it starts from a young age with media, family and environment and looks like this: in order to be enough you are expected to be kind. Be polite. Put others before yourself. Don't be dramatic. Don't make a scene. Speak up, but not too loudly and only if it won't upset anyone. Does this sound archaic? If you think so, you'd be surprised at how many current college women say they feel it. Remember when I said many of us are more afraid of embarrassment than dying? Yep, that plays a part, too. Don't misunderstand me, I don't believe these things are ill-intended, or even necessarily all bad. But if we are taught about the expectations of appropriate representation and not *also* taught the importance of boundaries, the importance of speaking up when we feel something isn't right, then these filters can lead to a woman responding in an unhealthy way, and sometimes in dangerous circumstances. The importance of saying, "You're making me uncomfortable," and believing that our comfort is as important as the other person's, is huge. Simply being empowered with the understanding that "No," is a complete sentence can go a long way. You see, as women, we are taught from a young age to compete and compare. We are often referred to as "cute" or "beautiful" more often than "smart" and "innovative". We long for acceptance, approval, and love, so we naturally gravitate toward what has given us this sense of belonging in the past. Young women who use their sexuality to gain attention are often actually seeking *belonging* from somewhere aligned with their childhood narrative: Your worth is in your looks. The media *certainly* doesn't help this. Did we ever get over the Carl's Jr. commercial with the near-naked woman eating a burger while the sauce drips down her cleavage and onto a car? Are the Grammy's any better? Over-sexualizing women is not empowerment, friends. It reinforces to those already objectifying us that *that* is where our value lies, when they instead need help understanding that we are more than that. This lie is reinforced everywhere we look and can come in a million different packages. We are taught to compare. No wonder we strive to achieve unachievable expectations. The point of this is not to place blame or identify as victims, but rather to see that knowledge is power and manipulation is real. Discovering our filters allows us to expose them. Exposing our filters allows us to reject them, and to reject them empowers us to speak about them. Sharing them with others who may not realize how influenced they are by harmful beliefs and the self-inflicted expectations that come with them, can start a powerful ripple effect. So what is the root problem here? Yes, media, culture and community—but what can these beliefs not exist without? *Comparison.*

When I speak publicly, I often show a picture of crabs in a bucket. Do you know why you never have to put a lid on a bucket of crabs? Because crabs, by nature, will pull each other down whenever one gets close to escaping. Sisters. Friends. Is this not what we do to one another? Are we secretly only cheering for those who we consider behind us, or those in different arenas and thus not a threat to our glory? **"Empowered Women Empower Women." I love the sentiment, but do we *really*? Or are our seemingly confident behaviors driven by the insecurity that tells us our worth is dependent on being better than someone else—which leaves us no choice but to compare?**

In conversations about women's empowerment with large groups of students, what often comes up is the idea that when competitiveness is triggered in us, it can result in actions that don't align with the values we profess to carry. Instead, we believe the lie that we are only good enough if we are somehow better than someone else. So in our insecurity we choose to invest in comparison rather than accomplishment in order to find validation that we are worthy of acceptance. There's a lot of reflection required if we are going to truly start empowering one another, and that requires us choosing to champion openness and compassion. **When we don't believe there's room for all of us, and we categorize ourselves as better or worse than others without knowing their full story, no one wins**. When we say things like, "I'm not like other girls," or find ways to put other women down to elevate ourselves, we gain the illusion of worthiness or superiority. Do we believe we are pretty because we get more attention than another? Or simply because we take care of ourselves and *choose* to like the way we look? Do we believe we are smart because our grades or jobs are better than someone else's grades or job, or because we know we are good problem-solvers and are committed to learning? Why do we do this to Womanhood? We shouldn't have to compare and focus on others' failures in order to believe we are worthy of love and belonging.

I believe we are better than this. We are all capable of greatness. Every. Single. One of us. But first, we have to get out of our own way and start believing it so that our actions *show* support rather than our words merely *saying* we support. The problem with finding our value in being better than others is that the rat race will never end. Comparison steals our joy. My husband jokes that, "The first thing you learn when you buy a boat is there's always someone with a bigger boat." If you let your "boat" define your worth, nothing will ever be enough. It's the same way in career industries. Whether it's becoming CEO or a top influencer, if status is the end-all-be-all that defines your worth, just wait until you feel the pressure and disappointment of achieving it. That type of fulfillment won't last; as soon as you get there, you have to start worrying about staying there, because as Heidi Klum on Project Runway says, "One day you're in, and the next you are out." Finding our worth in achievement alone also leaves no room to celebrate the milestones along the path—it only focuses on the peak moments and ignores all of the hard work and stumbles that got you there. It's those stumbles and in-the-trenches moments that build our character, strength, and integrity. They're critical parts of our journey. Achieving status will always leave us empty if our worth is dependent on it.

What if it doesn't have to be this way? Is it possible to fully chase purpose over status, and cheer for one another whole heartedly without anything being taken away from us? Yes! Yes, it is. If we can stop buying into the belief that we are only enough if we are better than others, then self-confidence will come so much easier. Insecurity cannot exist without comparison.

Can you imagine the world we would live in if we truly believed there was room for us all? **Breaking free from comparison culture would mean we no longer live with** insecurity, only difference. **We could then trade in comparison for celebration** *of* **our differences. Creating a world where women believe we can all succeed and that your success no longer equals my failure would mean complete** *freedom.* Choosing to make this shift will bring us to a place of pure, powerful, beautiful empowerment of ourselves and one another.

Download your Workbook
Pages for Comparison here.

For a Desktop Experience, go to:
CollegeMoxie.org/how-to-find-your-moxie

4

COMPASSION

D uring my junior year of college, I became the president of my sorority. I came in with fresh energy and a lot of ideas that I believed would keep us strong and make us even better. Had you asked me if I had a wide perspective of my campus culture, I would have emphatically answered in the affirmative.

I became friends with other chapter presidents, one of which I became particularly close to. Walking home from a meeting one day, I proudly announced to my new friend that since we were only allowed to have five Exchanges (theme parties with a fraternity) per semester, that our sorority was going to intentionally have four with the usual suspects we socialized with, and one would be with a fraternity that we didn't really know. This was our way of making sure we weren't being too exclusive and were expanding our Greek relations to ensure we would continue to be open-minded as to who we were hanging out with. (I'm cringing as I write this to relive how "woke" I believed my plan was.)

My new friend thought for a minute and responded by telling me that she continues to tell *her* members this: "If we each commit to meeting three new people a day, then eventually we will be asked to an Exchange." Inside I died a little as I realized how skewed, limited, and privileged my perspective had been. Here I thought I was doing such a noble thing for our community, when in reality I had absolutely no concept of what another's experience was every single day, longing for the opportunity to socialize in the way we were willingly limiting.

I felt terrible and my shock was obvious. I wanted to help but didn't know how. What happened next though, sticks with me. "You don't need to feel bad for us," she said. "It's good for us to meet new people and I see my women becoming more confident in doing so." I breathed a sigh of relief. My friend had compassion for *me*; for my ignorance and my flippant comments that moments before I had been so proud of. I will never forget this conversation because of how she met me where I was, saw my heart and assumed positive intent. She saw me and she loved me, and she let me know that my perspective was not everyone's. What's more, she did it kindly by leading with love.

We currently live in a world where it's easy to assume negative intent. In fact, our culture tries to insist that we emphatically judge one another based on a single decision, headline, or tweet when we never have all the facts. We've lost both our willingness to love people in their humanness and to call them up to do better. It's no wonder that cancel-culture brings with it a severe increase in mental health challenges for our young people. Perfect isn't real and we all need grace sometimes.

It's dangerous to lose our compassion and forget that we *all* have room for improvement. Choosing to have compassion for fellow flawed humans is a crucial part of any healthy relationship or community. We *all* have things to learn and will hopefully always grow and evolve. If we don't allow for others' humanness to be part of us, choosing to believe we all have room for growth, then we are essentially saying we give up on people to ever be more tomorrow than they are today.

Can you see the irony in losing compassion for someone who you don't believe is compassionate enough? Or saying that your beliefs are not going to tolerate opposition when simply asking questions and truly seeing one another can help us understand where each other is coming from? Maybe we'd learn that no one person is a single label. How much more understanding might we have if we simply decided to care about someone else's journey as much as our own?

All of our beliefs, convictions, and values come from our own personal experiences- and here's the kicker: no two of us have shared all of the same ones. Even twins experience circumstances of life very differently. You and I might make similar choices and end up with very different consequences, for better or worse. In our ability to sit behind a screen and judge each other with clicks and taps, based on tiny fragments of information, we fail to connect with the eyes—the soul—of the human we are categorizing, labeling, and judging.

I want to understand other people's stories. Don't we all desire to be *known*? **I think our greatest human need is to be known: to feel seen and to be understood, and feel certain that if we were to leave this life, it would matter to someone. When we put people in boxes and make harsh judgements about them, we are acting in direct contradiction to love and tolerance. What if instead we decide that we are brave enough to seek discomfort and invest in discovering someone else's 'why'?**

Here's how that could look: "Oh, that is what you believe? What led you to that? What have you experienced that is *different from my life experience* that causes you to view the events of the world through your unique lens? I want to understand your 'why,' your personal motivation and your purpose. Are you willing to share it with me?" Doesn't this prove to be so much harder than it sounds? It doesn't have to be.

When we recognize that we are flawed and that even in our most imperfect state we hold value, we can then accept that others do, too. It is also helpful when leaning into discovery and discomfort to first guard our minds and invest in things that are good for us, so that our roots grow deep. When our mental, physical, and spiritual self-care are on point, we are less likely to flail in the wind and take the bait when gaslit by headlines or relatives or whatever does it for us.

Leaning into knowing those who disagree with us takes courage and self-awareness. But when we know who we are and *like* who we are enough to *love* who we are—flaws and all—our self-worth detaches from the outcome of someone else's words. We then open ourselves up to *learning* from and appreciating one another's differences, rather than allowing them to splinter our communities.

The intersection of love and learning is where compassion lives. That is where relationships and understanding thrive. We can't control ours or anyone else's circumstances. But we *can* always control how we respond and whether we choose to *be* love.

Our focus is another choice within our control. We can choose to care only about ourselves and what benefits us, or we can choose to share the stage and believe that we are enough the way we are and decide to have compassion for others. People in need, people who struggle with how to treat others, people in leadership...we *all* need compassion.

For many years, I've volunteered for my international sorority, and it has taught me a million valuable things. How to be a leader, how *not* to be a leader. How large organizations are run, and that there is *always* more than you know. For a year I took on the responsibility of being a Risk Management and Policy Specialist for every chapter in California, Arizona, and New Mexico, which tasked me with assessing and mitigating high-risk activities and holding members and chapters accountable for said actions. It was the worst job in the entire world, and if any of you know someone who has this job, I suggest you give them a big fat hug, STAT.

It's hard being the presenter of punitive consequences; there is nothing joyful about laying down the law when all you have is authority and no relationship. I often felt misunderstood, hopeless, and defeated in my attempt to help those I oversaw to see the bigger picture. The biggest ah-ha moment I had was realizing that beneath every high-risk behavior is a human with a story. Behavior egregious enough to put me on a next day flight was often the cry for help of a young woman already riddled in shame.

My approach softened. I became more interested in who they were and what their story was rather than seeing them as a single behavior. My leadership skills grew immensely as I learned that it is possible to lead with love, speak with respect, and still engage with truth. These are now the principal values of College Moxie.

Speaking the truth in love is hands down, one of the hardest things I have ever been asked to do. It sounds easy, but it isn't. Being loving and kind—simple. Speaking truth—simple! But to speak truth in a vulnerable, caring way that might not be received well and lead to personal rejection is, oh, so much harder.

If you want to be a change-maker and culture shifter with courageous moxie you can't do it without compassion—it simply can't be done. You can tell people what to do and call it leadership (I used to do that, too, by the way). But if you *truly* want to make a difference and want others to follow you, compassion matters. No one cares about following a leader that doesn't show care for the people they lead. When we approach people who disagree with us with openness and compassion, we increase the health of our communities and our relationships. We feel more connected to others and become more understanding of our differences. This doesn't mean we have to become tolerant of all behaviors or start agreeing with everyone; it just means we choose to remember that we are more than one decision we've made and so are they.

We all make bad decisions, some more publicly than others. My hope is that *when* we do, we have people in our lives who are willing to call us up instead of out. Friends who will risk that awkward moment and say, "I love you and I believe you are better than this. Here's where your perspective might be limited. I hope you make a different decision next time. How can I help you do that?" Compassion and accountability will always triumph over trying to shame someone into change. Shame limits people. And when our confidence is rocked, we become even more likely to make bad decisions.

Being the one who is confronted with love and support isn't always easy, either. But would it be kind for a doctor to tell you that everything is fine rather than that you have cancer when you do? Nope. No it would not. When we choose to speak the truth in love, our words cast hope. We are letting someone know we believe in them, see their potential, and know that they are more than the sum of the worst decisions they've made.

We are all works in progress and when one of us is told we are beyond repair, growth, or hope, a very sad thing takes place: we start to believe it. Our confidence dims. We sit paralyzed in shame and become self-absorbed, focused on everything we wish was different, sometimes trying desperately to project our anger onto the world so we don't have to believe it was our own decisions that led us to exactly where we are. How would it be different if, instead, someone told us we were seen in our most flawed state and still loved and capable of more?

Insecurity cannot exist without comparison. Authentic community cannot exist without compassion. We must each get to know ourselves and become comfortable with who that is in order to allow others to know us, also. Accepting these truths means you are no longer in your own way and that self-care no longer has to border on self-absorption because *you are already enough*. When we remove comparison, compassion becomes easier, too, because when we see value in every human experience, we will naturally want to bring both similar and different people into our circles.

My journey isn't in the way of your journey. My *purpose* isn't in conflict with your purpose. What I've learned and lived doesn't trump the validity of your experiences, just as yours don't trump mine. Do you need help along your path? I'll help you. Do you have goals and dreams that are similar to mine? I'll *still* help you. You made a mistake that you paid for publicly? I'm still here. If we start to lean into grace and collaboration and see the benefit of our collective experiences, we will not only feel free from comparison but also experience the joy that comes from helping one another. And here's an added bonus: leaning into compassion both requires and *produces* confidence.

When I'm having a rough day or a sad moment, my favorite thing to do is sneak onto our College Moxie Instagram account and "throw up love" on women's posts. (That's what we call it.) I tell them they're beautiful, that they're amazing, and I encourage them to keep up the good work and keep shining bright. Every single time I do this, I feel better. Choosing to take the focus off of ourselves and onto encouraging others instead, automatically shifts my sense of purpose.

When we have purpose, we see our own worth. We love ourselves more. And when we love ourselves more, we can more easily love others. Confidence breeds compassion, which in turn breeds more confidence and willingness to invest in community with those who may not share our beliefs or views. Compassion is vital to how we expand our circles and exposure to others, therefore increasing both our ability to learn and influence.

Download your Workbook
Pages for Compassion here.

For a Desktop Experience, go to:
CollegeMoxie.org/how-to-find-your-moxie

5

CONTROL

'm currently writing this from a hotel room in Indianapolis after the first weekend of March Madness. My father is the athletic director at a small division 1, non-football school in Tulsa, Oklahoma. Their men's basketball team has made it into the NCAA Tournament for the first time in 13 years, and just won its second game in the tournament—a feat not achieved since 1974.

To get here, the team had grabbed a record-breaking win against the number two seeded Ohio State, then again against Florida in the second round. This is an exciting, monumental event simply by this team beating the odds, but what makes it even more special is that my dad is retiring soon. He took the job 26 years ago, and through sheer blood, sweat, and tears, built the program back to an exciting, respectable division 1 program. The culmination of persistence, tireless hard work, a willingness to make difficult decisions, and an eye for smart hires, just became an international television phenomenon.

Against Ohio State, the players were calm and confident on the court against a team twice their size. They worked hard, and they worked together, never giving up hope that they could win. As I sat in the stands as purely a spectator, I couldn't help but believe that the outcome of this game might actually be somewhat determined by my commitment as a fan and my willingness to yell and cheer.

Of course, I was invested and wanted them to win. And because I wanted it and believed it could happen, I also believed there must be something I could do to help *make* it happen. I caught myself in this very silly belief I had clung to. As superstitious as coaches that don't change their socks, I actually believed that my effort could somehow make a difference somewhat equal to the players' efforts. If you're not already, you are now free to laugh.

Our "need" to be in control is another lie we believe that doesn't benefit us. Even when life circumstances make us feel like we are spiraling out of control, life is *actually* no different than it was prior to the new circumstances. We are always vulnerable; we just don't acknowledge it when things are easy. Life before 2020 only *felt* more predictable. My belief that if I didn't cheer hard enough then the team might not pull off a win is as silly as me believing I control the outcome of anything else circumstantial in my life. Yet it isn't something any of us usually want to admit.

I tend to equate control with safety. The myth goes like this: "If I am in control, then I cannot be upset nor harmed." If we have the illusion of control, we can better guarantee met expectations. But striking a balance between working toward our goals with passion and commitment, and setting ourselves up for constant disappointment, is a fine line here. We will likely exhaust ourselves and our relationships if we are constantly trying to control others and our circumstantial outcomes.

Growing up, my dad used to say, "When you get squeezed will you be a lemon or an orange? Because what you put in is what will come out." This has proven to be true in my lifetime after time. When I respond with patience, compassion, and understanding to a situation I cannot control, there's a good chance that before the incident, my self-care was on point. I've likely been eating well, getting some exercise and adequate good sleep. I've probably been spending time with people who fill my soul and lift me up. Listening to music, podcasts, and books that enrich and motivate, also feeds me in a nurturing way. All of these are things that cause "sweet juice" to come out when I'm squeezed by life.

In contrast, if I am not taking good care of myself: eating poorly, working without breaks for exercise and sunshine, not spending quality time with my family and friends, and upsetting the balance of my life, there's a good possibility I'm going to have a "sour," knee-jerk reaction when things don't go my way. I like the lemon and orange analogy because it brings perspective to the concept of control. **It isn't that we can't control *anything*, but rather focusing on what we *can* control is how we prepare to handle the things that are *out* of our control.** I want to meet adversity with kindness and compassion rather than bitterness and anger. It makes life easier for both myself and those around me.

I like to think of people as similar to trees. The roots are most important, but they are also the part you don't see. The leaves, branches and trunks are affected by what's going on beneath the surface, and only sometimes are the results visible. When our roots are deep and well-nourished, the trunk is stable and able to remain rooted and survive when harsh winds and hurricanes show up. What we choose to feed our roots, matters.

Our desire for control is best harnessed in making good choices for our roots and setting ourselves up to be strong mentally, physically, and emotionally; because trying to control our circumstances will always set us up for failure. There will always be things that happen that we don't expect, couldn't have predicted and can't avoid. Controlling our *response* to those events is what can help us to keep getting back up to face another wave when the surf pounds harder instead of giving up or drowning.

When I'm spending time in balance and surrounded by people who are good for me, I'm pretty good at rolling with the punches. But even in the stands of an unfamiliar school I didn't attend, I felt that my involvement mattered greatly. I attribute this to a couple of things. One, we sometimes think we are more important than we are. We all have the ability to carve a path to be change makers and put good into the world, but as main character syndrome suggests, not everything needs our involvement or opinions. Have we become a self-absorbed society that, because of the power of social media, has come to believe that our opinion is welcomed, important, superior and always necessary? Are we only interested in educating others on all the ways we are right? No one cares how much you know until they know how much you care.

Control is Dumbo's feather. We think we need it, but we don't. We think it has magical power, but it doesn't. The existence of the unknown will always be greater than what we can control. The magic is found in gleaning learning opportunities from our circumstances, that add to our perspective and growth.

I often imagine my life can be represented by a huge tapestry. Most days I only get to see the backside: the chaotic pile of knots, jumbled and clumped together in no real formation or resembling anything meaningful or good. But every once in a while, the wind will blow and I'm able to see the other side. There, I get a glimpse of a beautiful picture that has come together- formed by opportunities, heartbreaks, decisions, forgiveness, pain, and triumph.

In those moments, I know that all things are capable of working together for good. Even the toughest, darkest of times can be utilized to create beauty if we will allow them to. Healed wounds that bring us wisdom and strength, and scars that show others they're not alone have power when we can see them as part of the bigger picture. Reassurance of no wasted pain. The revelation that had we been given the chance to control everything- if we could determine the outcome of every situation- we likely would have never chosen the moments that would make us strong. The moments that gave us platforms, purpose, and opportunities to encourage each other would likely not exist if it were all within our control.

When we choose to fuel ourselves with good things, we will crumble less. Our vision will broaden, and we will see things that happen as part of a connected tapestry, rather than an isolated circumstance. We will utilize that perspective to become strategic rather than reactionary. We will start to see that circumstances might be happening *for* us instead of *to* us.

I have learned that blessings can come in very weird packages. When we are open to possibilities, grounded in goodness, and confident in ourselves, it's easier to accept what is out of our control and navigate forward in an intentional way. Control becomes about how we will respond to life, rather than putting all of our focus on attempting to make events happen.

Download your Workbook
Pages for Control here.

For a Desktop Experience, go to:
CollegeMoxie.org/how-to-find-your-moxie

THINGS THAT EMPOWER
our
MOXIE

6

CONFIDENCE

One of my most meaningful experiences as an actress was when I worked on an FX miniseries called FEUD about the delicious rivalry between Betty Davis and Joan Crawford, played by Susan Sarandon and Jessica Lang, respectively. The series was created by the legendary Ryan Murphy, who also created Glee, American Horror Story, The Politician, and Rachet. He is an icon in the entertainment industry, and to work on one of his creations that was limited to eight episodes was a huge honor.

To add to the exclusivity of this experience, Mr. Murphy also insisted on having at least half of his episodes directed by women, and he personally only directs one or two—one of which I was in. He is a fierce trailblazer in the industry for his stylistic eye and attention to detail as he beautifully unfolds and entwines storylines. As is the case for many successful humans, he is also known for having high standards and a low tolerance for not meeting the bar.

The project was top secret, so in old-school fashion, my script was delivered to me via FedEx, with only the pages of my scenes attached and everything irrelevant to my part blacked out. I scanned the pages for what I could decipher, between Sharpie lines and squiggles of knowledge I was not privy to, only to make a frightening discovery: I had no lines. I had, of course, auditioned with lines, an entire scene of them. I had to prove that I could convincingly speak with a British accent and mimic the mannerisms of a well-known, famous actress in the 40's.

I started to panic because I knew what this meant. It did not mean that I wouldn't be speaking in the show; it meant that I would not be able to show up *prepared* for what I would be speaking in the show. Being unprepared was (and is) one of my biggest fears. As someone diagnosed with Attention Deficit Disorder, I depend on the time to prepare in my own way and committing to my routine always meant more likelihood of ensuring success. I also appreciated the external validation that came with my preparedness that I really was great at this acting thing. *I* knew I was great at it, but spoken approval and validation from others was rare. Criticism, on the other hand, was crushing and easy to come by.

I often wonder now as I speak on campuses and hear other women's stories: *Are we in pursuit of perfectionism, not because we care so much about the quality of our work, but rather because if we are seen as "perfect," we can avoid criticism altogether?* Have we really tied constructive feedback so tightly to rejection that we are chasing something unattainable in order to avoid the possibility of being told we are human?

I'm not a parent, nor can I imagine the pressure of feeling responsible for the success or failure of another human life, only to be expected to let that go and allow them to grow, stumble, and learn on their own. I'll never claim to be an expert there. What I *can* tell you is that I see the consistent effect it has on young people today, and I fear that we are robbing them of the ability to tolerate discomfort. They are protected from conflict while pressured to be overachievers.

The same well-meaning adults who want them to avoid pain or having to work through difficulties, can also cause them to feel like they're failing. There is so much pressure to be perfect and they feel their worth is tied to an unachievable thing, so much that they are imploding at the idea of not being enough.

If you only take one thing away from this book, I hope it will be this: "Perfect" isn't real. It's not a thing. It has never been a thing. It is a myth and a lie that we buy into that not only sets us up for failure, but also those around us. Remember when I talked about the photo effects created from airbrush and contour apps? Not real. Someone's red carpet movie star life? Not the whole story, and not real. Someone's success story that doesn't include a bunch of failures? Not. Real.

So, what would happen if we flip the script and decide that constructive criticism is a *compliment*? What would be different if, in safe spaces with people who value us, we started to see constructive feedback as a gift because it meant someone saw our potential for growth? That they want us to be our best *and* be able to learn from their experiences? What an honor that someone would take the time to let us know how we can improve rather than just giving up on us all together.

When our self-worth is tied to the myth that we can make others believe we are perfect, we miss out on life itself. We don't know if our friendships are authentic. We don't give others the opportunity to show up for us, letting us know they see us, know us, and still love us. **Allowing perfection to be a standard for ourselves or others only sets us all up for failure**.

I showed up to set on my first day of filming FEUD, to find a new copy of the same marked up pages waiting for me in my trailer. I went into makeup, then hair. Still, no new script. I had to focus on being in the moment so that the pressure didn't cause me to crumble or panic. I reminded myself that it wasn't every day that Susan Sarandon and I were getting our makeup done two feet from each other while her little dog, Penny, explored the trailer. We chatted about Penny and Susan's latest activist work until I was called to set and introduced to the man I would be doing my scenes with.

Mr. Murphy approached us with a large book saying, "So I realized we need to be doing scenes from this play. Choose a few from different points and we will do those … in about 30 minutes." My brain says [insert the big-eyed panic emoji next to the poop one.] But I heard my mouth say with a smile, "Okay, sure!" I almost gave *myself* a look. Was I nuts? Was I just going to stay cool and act like it wasn't a big deal? Yes. Yes, indeed, I was. And, why? Because I only had two choices: make it about me, get lost in my feelings, and probably implode, OR focus on the task at hand, do it scared, and see what happened.

It was like winning the lottery to be standing there in the first place. Many people don't realize that just to get an audition for a studio or network project, odds are about one-in-five-hundred- a big deal. To then be called back to audition for the producers (which makes your chances of booking the part about 25-33% which is *still* not likely), and then be the ONE to *book* the role? Unicorns fly through the sky when it happens for us actors, and we don't take it lightly. So, yes. I decided to do it scared.

I often think of what might have been different in my younger years had I had the boldness to approach other things the same way. If I had run full force into challenges, instead of giving 95 percent—which was often good enough, but when it wasn't, I had that last 5 percent to blame as what could have made the difference. But if I didn't fully give my all, then I could never actually be rejected, it would just become a matter of needing to try harder. In other words, something I could control.

I spent so much time striving to be enough and to appear to have it all together, because appearance held greater value than vulnerable authenticity. Perhaps this is an unspoken midwestern value. But it's exhausting to strive. Confidence comes much more easily when you can *respect* those around you, but don't *need* their approval.

Back on set, I pulled it together and remembered, this wasn't the first time I had been under pressure to perform. My scene partner still had to finish getting his beard put on, but as soon as he was ready, it would be go-time. I saw the panic start to rise in him, too.

"I've got this. Can you trust me?" I said to a person I had met five minutes before, and miraculously he said, "Yes." I quickly flipped through the script and found three points in the timeline that made the most sense for that point in the story. I scanned to see where there were chunks of dialogue that were meaningful, but that could be delivered like popcorn- bite sized. Neither of us had time to memorize a monologue, and it was important to me that we were both equally set up for success.

I marked the pages and took off for the hair trailer. He reviewed and approved, and we practiced our three scenes for the entire 20 minutes we had, all while making sure my British accent and inflection came together with the new words on the page. Susan Sarandon watched us without comment. No pressure! We were called to set as four or five hundred period-dressed background actors filled the theater and a spotlight suddenly blinded me. Showtime.

When performing, in the wings of anything new, there are always butterflies. But when "Action!" is called, a shift takes place. There's no longer room for any "what-ifs" in the thought process, and fear of potential failure disappears because the future-focus is gone. It is now the present. It's time for action. Action requires being present, acting and responding, and that's *it*. When we choose to take action, we are choosing to move forward one step, one choice, one moment at a time.

What if we never moved forward and just stayed in the wings? Might we convince ourselves that busyness is equivalent to productivity? The human brain is a powerful thing, and we can convince ourselves of most anything if we try hard enough. So why not step away from self-limiting beliefs and step into fear?

When I feel afraid or in over my head, I look back to see where I've been. In the moment, it's easy to feel inadequate because all that is before us exists in the unknown. There's incredible power in looking back to remember the hurdles we've jumped, the boulders we've dodged, and the mountains we've climbed. We are *all* overcomers. We *all* have reasons to believe in ourselves. If you are reading this, your survival rate of bad days to-date is 100%. Confidence comes from taking action. And every time we take a step into the unknown, we reinforce that doing things scared does not kill us. It actually *empowers* us to overcome fear.

The freedom that comes from ditching comparison translates into endless possibilities. I rocked playing Margaret Leighton in that show. Susan Sarandon and Ryan Murphy both told me how talented I was. And you know what? It was different this time. I appreciated their feedback very much. They didn't have to say it, and I was very grateful that they chose to. But either way, it wasn't going to change how I felt about myself. I *knew* I had worked hard. *I* knew I had stepped up and delivered. And I knew that I could be proud of the work I had done because I gave it my ALL.

I am now at a place where I am able to fully love who I am, knowing that I am beautifully flawed, and that I will continue to make mistakes but that those mistakes do not define me. I no longer allow others to define my worth. My confidence comes from knowing myself, knowing my work ethic, committing to growth, and surrounding myself with people who are there for me. I no longer have room to fear being misunderstood. I no longer make time to stack my successes up against someone else's. I'm simply committed to being the best version of myself that I can be during each day that I'm given. And *that* gives me a lot more time to put action to things that matter.

Download your Workbook
Pages for Confidence here.

For a Desktop Experience, go to:
CollegeMoxie.org/how-to-find-your-moxie

7

CONVICTION

T here's a verse in the Bible that I don't particularly care for that says, "With much knowledge comes much grief." It's because it's so real that I don't enjoy it.

I sometimes envy people who think simply, don't dream big dreams, or who don't believe that they can change the world. Knowledge often causes us to see the dark tunnels underneath Disneyland that we all wish did not exist. I see this in my nephews who are brilliant beyond my own comprehension. It's mesmerizing to witness their extraordinarily complex thoughts as they question the inner workings of something almost immediately upon discovering its existence.

Not long ago, I found myself in a deep conversation with two of them about anxiety. I'm not sure it's possible for brilliant or ambitious people to not fight feelings of anxiousness sometimes—perhaps because we know and understand too much for our own good. Another Bible verse says, "To whom much is given much is required." I like this one much better because it creates an empowerment piece to the harsh side of the first, and I am always looking for what is actionable.

Action allows us to make a difference and matter. Action keeps us from feelings of failure or helplessness, because action is what we can *do*. Our world, our country and individuals have large, complex problems. How can we take sustainable and useful action? This sounds like such an overwhelming question with impossible answers, that I must remember the commitment I've made to keep my focus on what is within my control and what is positive. If I can boil things down to those categories, it's always easier to, as my good friend (and brilliant therapist) Fran Carona, Ph. D says, "feel my feet on the ground," then determine my choices.

Conviction often drives our motivation to want to have moxie—to be bold, to stand up and speak up, even if it might involve rejection. There are a million and one problems I would like to solve in the world, and figuring out where I personally can contribute, keeps my life peaceful, my head balanced, and helps me sleep at night despite the things I cannot change.

I don't believe it's right to ever leave someone in victimhood. We have to empower one another to utilize the skills we each have. To walk in purpose in order to *feel* purpose. Teaching someone skills so they can be self-reliant, contribute to their lives and society, feel good about their efforts, and not feel like their existence is a burden to others, brings hope. It brings confidence, and it brings joy.

Young women need to be taught not to allow their perceived failures to keep them in a mindset of unworthiness, because that results in comparison and toxic versions of competition. When I look at my life thus far, there have been many pivotal moments. There have been accomplishments, like getting to work on big studio films and TV shows and being recognized for my work with college women. Waiting to find and then marrying the man of my dreams.

But then there were also others. My brothers' death and the unraveling of my family. Surviving sexual assault. Feelings of loneliness and disrepair that resulted in me fully believing that God had taken the wrong kid throughout years of my adulthood. Big, brutal, heart wrenching events that I could have allowed to define me—and perhaps rightfully so. But there is no joy in feeling helpless. There was no hope or confidence or self-love that existed in me during those times, since *purpose* didn't exist in me.

Finding purpose and conviction to act on that purpose changed everything and allowed me to break free from the chains of comparison that held me back. What started with me simply being present as a twenty-something sorority advisor who didn't think she had much to offer, grew into finding my own purpose as I realized that other women in college wanted to share their struggles and experiences, and I could authentically share back. I learned that by choosing to be brave and to simply "do it scared," (another Fran quote) that I was able to help others. I don't believe in wasted pain. In fact, I'm passionate about eliminating the myth that pain is wasted time.

Everything I have been through and will go through in my life, I commit to eventually using to help others. This is *how* I can be part of the solution to humanity's many problems. *This* takes me from victim to empowered, because the choice of what I do with it is within my control. I can take my pain, choose to heal and grow from it, and then, when the wounds have healed and scars have sealed, I can present them to others as evidence they are not alone. My pain, my tragedy, my unfair circumstances can become powerful tools to speak to the power of community and make the world a better place.

Speaking authentically and leading with vulnerability in sharing our personal stories can be scary. It hasn't always been easy for me to talk about sexual assault or abandonment issues or feeling alone and finding comfort in the wrong relationships. These are deep—sometimes dark—vulnerable, challenging parts of me. But every time I choose to share my stories to empower others, I too am empowered. I am reminded that what I choose to spend my time doing is making a difference. Bravery uncovers the lies that say our dark, hidden spots make us unworthy of love, relationship and belonging. Bravery speaks directly to fear and takes away its power. Shifting perspective from helplessness to hero-ness (yes, I just made up that word, but I like it) puts us above it. Choosing bravery gives us the freedom to determine how we will utilize our experiences to influence rather than how we will respond to their control. Our chosen mindset in every moment matters. There is enormous power in no longer allowing our circumstances to determine who we are.

If you feel inspired to share your experiences with others, I want to encourage you in this: First, as the amazing researcher and author Brene Brown says in her book, Rising Strong, "Share from your heart, not your hurt." Don't share from an open wound. Share from a healed one. Don't push to share the things that you haven't yet dealt with. Doing so likely won't have as powerful an impact because you haven't yet learned all that you will learn, once you get some distance from it and see it as a single piece of you, rather than all of you. Another potential side effect of early sharing is creating unnecessary scarring for yourself and putting the responsibility of your healing on the audience who now feels they are in a therapy session. Share when you feel it is part of your past and not your present. Then, when you're ready to charge forth with the vision of letting others know they're not alone, just do it scared.

Download your Workbook Pages for Conviction here.

For a Desktop Experience, go to:
CollegeMoxie.org/how-to-find-your-moxie

8

CONTENTMENT

About ten years ago, I cut off contact with one of the closest friends I've ever had. She did some things that were unethical and possibly illegal for personal financial gain, and because of how close we were, people started to question my integrity and involvement, as well. I was devastated by every aspect of this situation. I asked for proof of the accusations made against her, and when I saw it in black and white, I knew distancing myself was the only safe thing to do. I wrestled with a range of emotions as I tried to make sense of a situation where I felt betrayed, sad, angry, judged, and stupid. How in the world had this happened, and who was this person I thought I knew so well?

I used to think I had to have all the answers. (This was back when I believed that perfect was real and somehow achievable, too.) So naturally, situations like this one caused me to deeply question my own judgement and sometimes feel really dumb. Looking back, however, I always knew she and I had different codes of ethics; I just didn't want to admit it because I felt guilty and judgmental when I tried. Admitting it would also conflict with what I wanted from our friendship, which was her company that I greatly enjoyed.

But over the years, there were several questionable instances where she would justify her inappropriate actions if money was at stake or there was a way for her to come out on top. On the other hand, she was also a really wonderful friend to me at times when others weren't and made a point to have my back in ways she didn't have to. Feeling fully seen and loved by her meant so much to me that I was crushed when I knew I needed a separation. I felt like I abandoned her and also felt abandoned *by* her. Throughout our friendship, I tried my best not to judge her, because our backgrounds were different and I saw the good in her, despite the bad. We were able to be very honest with each other, and we had shared great conversations about ethics and where her strong desire for materialism had originated. We were close, *close* friends.

We also had some mutual friends (who were closer with her than me), who said things that made me feel judged and in the wrong for calling out issues and wanting to distance myself from these behaviors—which was impossible to do without distancing myself from her. The truth is that because no one is *all* good or *all* bad, I chose confusion when someone I considered good, did things I knew were wrong. I allowed others' opinion of me as "judgmental," to influence my sense of worth and my moral compass, instead of confidently standing in black and white truth and speaking up for it. I hated the stress of this and hated feeling misunderstood even more.

The peace that I felt after time and distance was equally crushing, because I had hoped it would be temporary and I didn't want to lose my friend. My gut, however, knew that this was not a safe relationship for me. I knew that my love for her and my guilt by association were both dangerously close to a point of no return if I didn't maintain my boundaries. I knew I had done the right thing… and I felt horrible about it.

Finding contentment in circumstances that involve big feelings of conflict and disappointment is *really* hard. Finding contentment in anything that doesn't go our way can be hard, but it's also necessary for our growth and preparation for the next time something blindsides us. Everything has purpose if we look for it. Choosing to believe this gives me both hope and personal responsibility to grow from every situation. I also have to appreciate opportunities to look back and say, "You know what? I can choose to 'see what I see and know what I know' a little better next time."

I knew right from wrong. I felt the warnings … new friends she'd made who could justify most anything, were openly manipulative, and wore their self-serving pride like a badge of honor. I just didn't *want* to believe it. I had no involvement with what she had done, but I did have a responsibility to be honest with myself, find my own learning opportunity, and grow to establish different boundaries more quickly should I ever land in the same position again. **That's how I went from a victim in friendship to a woman empowered through painful, ugly circumstances.**

This concept of "being a good person" is confusing and problematic, because none of us are *all* good or *all* bad. It can be particularly damaging in terms of acknowledging sexual assault, because many women are assaulted by people they know or maybe even think of as a friend. Unraveling this can be extremely difficult because people with good qualities are also capable of doing really bad things. Magnifying people's positive qualities and minimizing their negative ones never serves us well. We have to be willing to face things head on and evaluate facts in order to have healthy relationships. This can only begin with having an honest, loving relationship with ourselves.

Whatever circumstances you find yourself in right now, no matter how challenging, discovering what can be learned from them and where you can improve is the quickest line to actionable empowerment. Where might you benefit from establishing boundaries in a relationship? Or in an extreme case, make the tough decision to end one altogether?

Taking a long hard look in the mirror and making these difficult decisions allows us to find contentment despite our circumstances. We go from victimhood to finding peace because our mindset shifts from life happening *to* us to us making choices that *empower* us in our own personal growth and ability to take action.

Who and what do you allow to define your worth? To whom do you give your power to dictate whether or not you're enough? As a visual creative, I like to think of myself as an apartment with many rooms. I get to decide to whom and what I will rent my space to each day- and there's only so much available room. If I rent my space to things I can't control: other people's problems, selective facts and assumptions, problematic relationships, judgements and negativity, then that will likely make my apartment a stressful, sad place to be, without a lot of resolution. If, however, I rent my space to things that bring me joy: safe relationships that build me up and won't ask me to compromise my character, places where I can contribute and give back, and things that are positive and within my control, then I have created a happy, peaceful space to exist, even if upsetting circumstances surprise me from time to time.

I used to rent space to worry when I felt misunderstood. I also used to rent space to insecurity because of the worry from *being* misunderstood. I hated the idea of someone thinking anything about me that wasn't true. But I don't anymore. Now, when I feel misunderstood, I reflect on which things are within my control to clarify, and which are not my responsibility to 'make' someone understand. It doesn't mean it's always easy to do, but my contentment comes in managing my own expectations. I now know that misunderstandings are inevitable in human-to-human relationships. Things happen. And when they do, my job is to determine what is worth my time and within my control and go from there. When we accept this, it is much easier to find contentment in life despite our circumstances. We become free to focus on purpose instead of flooding our apartments with worry, doubt, fear and "what if's." Freedom comes when we go with our gut regardless of what someone else might think.

Who and what we rent our space to is wholly important and essential to being our best selves. I am more confident and at peace when my world is balanced, and I am making good choices about what to allow into it. I have to be good at guarding my mind and not allowing an overflowing closet of circumstances to overtake my "apartment"—something that happens fast if left unchecked. Worry, fear, and doubt can throw a house party in a hot minute and before I know it, the entire apartment will be consumed with damage and chaos that takes much longer to clean up than it did to create.

My husband laughs that I like to watch old television shows like Leave it to Beaver before we go to sleep at night. For me, this is a simple way to guard my mind. I have a terribly imaginative dream life that can leave me with a range of negative feelings by morning based on things that in reality never happened. So when the conflict of an entire episode is fourteen cents missing from Wally's ice cream cart—yes, please! That's the only kind of problem I want to allow into my head before I drift off.

You may be laughing, but I make this choice because I know myself; I am a deeply impressionable empath. Because of this, I feel *all* the feels of others. Growing up, my parents couldn't watch the news on Wednesdays without a huge scene because if I saw the segment, "Wednesday's Waiting Child," there were going to be serious demands and a strong line of questioning about why the Carters could not provide a home for every single one of those kids who needed one. It devastated me to know that kids didn't have homes, and it still does. Because of this, I am intentional about helping where it's reasonable for me to, and then, guarding my mind once I can't.

I choose to focus on two things: what's positive, and what's within my control. In a world of a million problems, I have learned to discern where I can make a difference and put my focus there- not on the media hype of everything else that is sometimes intended to gaslight us more than inform us, but what action I can take to make a difference. Then, outside of that, I focus on what is positive. When I choose to guard my mind, I sleep well. I'm at peace when I wake up and have more focus and confidence to spend my day working toward making a difference. I dream big and make bold moves in spaces where I can make an impact, and along the way I keep a positive outlook because I know worrying won't change outcomes. I choose to be content. It doesn't mean everything is always positive, nor does it mean I avoid things that are real. It just means I choose to keep my headspace in those two places most often. When I start to become overwhelmed, I ask myself, "What is actionable, controllable, and positive?" and let go of the rest.

We are our own worst enemies when it comes to taking on feelings of failure and hopelessness. There have and always will be unknowns; a worldwide pandemic just made that fact glaringly obvious. Finding contentment beyond our circumstances is key to our happiness and our ability to find joy in the present moment. Doing so takes away our fears of unmet expectations and leaves more room for moxie. If we are always striving forward and lamenting back, we aren't able to savor the amazing joys and opportunities we have in daily life.

My husband and I choose vacation destinations based on what areas of the world have limited Wi-Fi availability. I know it's extreme and it's probably a bit sad that that's what it takes for us to disconnect, but it works for us. We are intentional about creating moments away from devices to enjoy time together and sit with whatever beauty might reveal itself in the present. Guarding our minds and not allowing life to overtake us is essential to protecting our headspace, energy, and outlook. I find contentment by acknowledging what there is to be grateful for in whatever present moment I find myself in. Whether in the calm of the storm or the eye of it, my outlook and level of contentment is always my choice.

Download your Workbook Pages for Contentment here.

For a Desktop Experience, go to:
CollegeMoxie.org/how-to-find-your-moxie

WAYS TO UTILIZE
our

MOXIE

9

COMMUNICATION

I used to think I didn't have a very good relationship with my dad when we lived in different places. My mom has always been my go-to phone call, whether I need a voice of reason or am stuck in a traffic jam. She and I can talk for hours about everything and nothing at all, and always find our conversations to be meaningful and hilarious.

My dad, however, is a man of few words here and there by text and often wonders if I need something when I call. This used to bother me and make me feel disconnected from him, until I realized it's just who he is. In person, he is always interested in my life. He's talkative, especially when a subject interests him, but even then he's more pensive and thoughtful. When I spent a week in Indianapolis with him and my mom for the infamous basketball games, I became his interim secretary of sorts. We drove several hours back and forth from Chicago, where I would read him hundreds of congratulatory texts and he would dictate his response. I am so grateful for those moments because they taught me something valuable: my dad can be completely moved by someone's words and say, "Wow. That was really kind. Write him back and say, 'Thanks John. Hope you're doing well'." And it would mean a lot. I loved having the opportunity to see his communication from the other side. When I had only been the recipient of the texts like, "Thanks, Lizz. Love you," it didn't feel like much in response if I had written lengthy, heartfelt messages. That day in the car, I realized that my assumptions had caused me to miss out on knowing how sincere and loving his responses were all those years.

Communication is so important in every aspect of our lives, yet can also be really tricky and confusing, especially in this age of electronics. We no longer have more face-to-face interactions than those with keyboards. We don't even hear one another's voices as often as we used to. To think of how many assumptions we are conditioned to make is baffling. How often do we try to predict, assume, and determine someone's tone of voice in texts? We're thinking, *was that genuine? Was it sarcastic? Am I being ignored?*

The other day, I was frustrated with my husband for not replying to a text I sent, but instead replying to the one I'd sent after. I had all but convinced myself that he was avoiding my thoughts on that part of our conversation, when I decided to call and ask. On the phone, he explained that he had been making himself dinner and had quickly replied to the most recent one he saw. Even as I write about the horrible, self-inflicted consequences of making assumptions, I still do it every day. Assumptions—another attempt at feeling in control—are never our friend if we are assuming the worst. Our imaginations are powerful things, and can also be our biggest enemies, if we don't keep ourselves in check.

When I went to therapy for depression years ago, my therapist taught me something great. When I feel overwhelmed, I am to make two lists. The first is a list of beliefs I have that are stressing me out. The other list is of hard facts and evidence that support those beliefs. I love this exercise and still do it, because it shows how very imaginative we are in creating assumptions about people, circumstances, and potential outcomes in an attempt to gain control. I realized that much of my anxiousness was caused by my own assumptions and wild imagination, rather than based on actual facts.

Leading with love can be hard. It requires vulnerability and sometimes feels counterintuitive. But to assume the best in people and choose to approach them in kindness, sets us up for so much more success than making negative assumptions and telling others to be ready to play defense. *How* we choose to communicate is just as important as *what* we choose to communicate. Healthy, respectful communication tools are weapons for good in any arsenal. From military handbooks to hostage negotiations, to speech writers and journalists, the words we choose matter and our integrity in them matters. We can easily sway people with our words. We can mislead, falsely represent, and create chaos in a single tweet, text, or Snap. We've all seen it done.

Recognizing the power of our words and how we use them, helps us connect with others in a way that builds trust and respect. We can either be tolerated, in the form of others halfway listening and keeping their mouth shut, or we can engage in productive conversations that can spark real change in both parties. Active listening is becoming a lost art. We are so quick to pounce when someone asks for an opinion that we lose sight of the opportunity to learn from others by listening. I believe the key to being a changemaker- to having moxie- is leading with love, leaning into discomfort, and allowing others to feel heard. By not making our voice the top priority in every conversation, we also put others at ease. They in turn will be more likely to express curiosity for our point of view, rather than feeling like a hostage to our opinions that are rooted in our specific experiences. Confidence and compassion make this much more possible because when we are at peace with ourselves, we are naturally less intimidated, less triggered, and less likely to be wounded by others. Puffer fish puff up and extend their scaly weapons at the first sign of an attack. How are we as humans doing with that?

Communication doesn't only mean expressing ourselves with words. We communicate whether we are open, friendly, confident, bitter, or challenging, nonverbally as well. We also teach others whether we are seeking learning opportunities or a platform to preach in every interaction. Choosing to respect others' points of view allows us to create safe spaces for open and honest dialogue in a way that shows the silent strength of our moxie, instead of having to scream from the rooftops that we have it. When we succeed in creating safe spaces for everyone to be honest, that's where deep, authentic connection happens. Vulnerability happens. Truthfulness happens- because the necessary trust was built.

And, here in this sacred place, we are given the privilege of seeing each other more intimately and the chance to gain incredible understanding of each other's hopes, dreams, and fears. This knowledge is a power to be cherished. When we can peer into the life and soul of another human to discover where their experiences have shaped their worldview, we now have the gift of truly knowing them. We gain a beautiful perspective. And we can now better understand how to approach them, and what might cause them to feel unsafe.

Being a strong communicator doesn't just mean expressing ourselves well. It also means allowing others to communicate and meeting them with openness. Creating safe spaces isn't easy, because as long as we are capable of having memories, we are capable of having baggage that can influence how we judge others. But when we invest in relationships and listen more than we speak, we gain the trust required and our moxie begins to speak for itself.

Download your Workbook
Pages for Communication here.

For a Desktop Experience, go to:
CollegeMoxie.org/how-to-find-your-moxie

10

COMMUNITY

'm a people person. I thrive off of the energy of others. I love hearing people's stories and learning about what makes them who they are. Throughout my life, I have always had multiple groups of friends. Growing up it was our neighborhood, our church, our country club, and my school that provided these. Each community brought me a different perspective, too.

I remember realizing around 7th grade that in school, I felt like we didn't have a lot of money, but at church, we seemed wealthy. I'm grateful to have always had the opportunity to learn from the good people in my life who came from different environments and walks of life. Learning about others' life experiences feeds my soul. Yet in all of this, I have rarely felt that I shared a movie-like closeness with anyone. I have always felt like I was part of the in-crowd but a bit on the outskirts. Perhaps it was because my parents had stricter rules than most of my school friends which didn't allow me to participate in everything my peers did, and our other communities were farther away. Maybe it was that I struggled with ADD and perhaps my perspective wasn't always accurate about my memories or relationships. I always knew people cared about me, but I'm not sure I've often felt *understood*.

The relationships in which I've come closest, however, have been deeply meaningful to me. One or two while growing up, a few in college and early adulthood, and a number of very special ones now. Timothy Keller once wrote: "To be loved but not known is comforting but superficial. To be known and not loved is our greatest fear." He included even more awesomeness in that paragraph of his book, *The Meaning of Marriage*, but this section strikes me deeply. I know how fortunate I am to have always known that I was, and am, loved. But to be seen and known and *still* loved is the thing we are all hoping for. We all want to be known and for that to be enough without having to put on a happy face and be the life of the party in order to be accepted. To be known in all our humanness- the good, the bad, the achievements and the shame- to be fully known and still loved is what our souls long for.

When I went off to college, I decided to start anew, but faking it became exhausting. Going through sorority recruitment, I decided to take a chance and be brave. I remember feeling comfortable enough in my discomfort to risk a really awkward moment. I worked up the courage to tell some women I had just met days before that I was not okay. I halfway expected them to just stare blankly back at me. Some of my closest friends in high school didn't know what to say when Scott died, so how in the world could I expect women I had just met to truly see me or understand? The beauty was, they didn't have to understand in order to see me. They let me *know* that they were with me at that moment and that they cared. They compassionately and genuinely said they were sorry and asked how they could support me. This was the first social experiment I conducted that proved I could be seen and cared about in a brand new community, without having it all together.

My heart needed this to prove true more than the rest of me will ever know. My brokenness ran so deep that I was desperate to feel seen and to still be enough in my broken state. The way these women, Gina, Emily, and Jen, responded to me during what I now understand is a high-pressure, tightly scheduled, and well-rehearsed day of meeting hundreds of people, caused me to believe in fresh starts and the possibility of healing. I saw firsthand the power of community, the power of being my authentic self, and feeling seen and known. I had proof that when given the opportunity to help, there are people who want to. Despite what we see in the media and in movies like Legally Blonde and Animal House, I fight for the sorority experience because mine changed my life. As women, we often have a tendency to think that whatever we are going through, we must be the only one going through it. We believe the lie that we are alone, and that no one else will understand. We believe that if they knew our flaws, they wouldn't accept us. But the truth is, we are made for community. We need community. There is *power* in community.

Perhaps that's why sometimes we choose unhealthy communities. I often wonder if college women—or maybe all of us at times—believe the lie that being in a mediocre relationship, or even a bad one, is better than being alone. Pressures we allow ourselves to feel, based on what we see on social media and in Rom-Coms, cause us to believe that we are only enough if we are surrounded by "friends" at all times— and lots of them. If our motive for seeking community is improving our appearance, then do we allow our subpar relationships and toxic friendships to hold space because we fear loneliness would be worse? I think so. Surrounding ourselves with people who will be *for* us is essential to our mental health and happiness. I now know that means I would rather have one good friend than five semi-safe friends.

In a movie I filmed called, *Catching Faith*, my now-friend Andrea Polnaszek, LCSW introduced me to a powerful activity that we now use in our ELEVATE curriculum during the "Safe Relationships" discussion with our chapters. Each person has three concentric circles, with the smallest representing what is closest to our heart. We put the names of people in our lives inside the circles and evaluate their placement to determine if anyone should be moved in or out.

Sometimes we find that people we consider friends have not proven to be safe with the most intimate details of our lives. Other times we find that there are people whom we initially don't consider *that* close, but who might be worth investing more time in because they have shown qualities of being a safe friend. I have learned the value of having fewer people in my inner circle. My time is more limited than it used to be, and I want to be intentional about where I am both investing in friendships and being filled—influenced—by them. People shift across our circles from time to time, and some people leave them altogether. I'm now old enough to know that that's not only *okay* but that sometimes it's actually good and healthy.

Boundaries are our friends. Being intentional about our communities keeps us in good, healthy headspaces. It also makes us better friends to others by ensuring that we are being fueled and encouraged by people who want what is good for us. Having healthy relationships also allows us to have more to give so we aren't left trying to pour from an empty cup.

I find that gratitude greatly impacts my sense of community as well. It is easy for me to take for granted my closest and safest relationships. There was much I took out on my mom in my younger years because I knew she would love me no matter what. Similarly, in my adult life, it's my closest humans who sometimes see the worst of me. When my patience is limited and I'm pushing back against community, I'm reminded to pause and list all that I'm grateful for: friends who love me, a patient and understanding family, volunteers who pour their energy and passion into *my* cause to help further our impact, and my own ability to work in my purpose every day.

When I take time to name out loud or list what it is that I'm grateful for, my attitude shifts, and humility replaces entitlement. The saying "gratitude transforms the attitude" is oh, so real. I often find myself becoming thankful for the opportunity to have the very things that frustrate me. It's the irony of life, isn't it?

Our willingness to hit the reset button on our very specific perspectives reminds us that we are not perfect and no one else is either. Listing gratitude also reminds me of how others accept me imperfectly and that I often need to adjust my expectations and do the same. When we cultivate gratitude, grace, and compassion in our communities, we allow them to safely grow in authenticity and richness.

Download your Workbook
Pages for Community here.

For a Desktop Experience, go to:
CollegeMoxie.org/how-to-find-your-moxie

11

CONTINUATION

J ust shy of a significant birthday, I accidentally met the man of my dreams at a restaurant bar on my way to a funeral, 45 miles from home. Our meeting circumstances were as unique as our relationship is, and I truly wouldn't change a thing. He is everything I ever hoped for: loving, intelligent, handsome, kind, strong, thoughtful, driven, full of integrity, and he makes me laugh every day. When he asked me to marry him 11 months later, it was an easy decision for me. My answer, however, also included another. I knew in my heart that it wasn't going to be best for us to have children. I believe if I had said I needed to have a child in order to be happy, that he loved me enough to comply. But I also loved *him* enough to not put him through it. He already has two grown children, and starting over likely would have aged us both in ways we didn't want to consider.

The night we got engaged, I began to think about the finality of this decision I was making and what it would look like for me. If I wasn't going to be a mom, then what did I want my legacy to look like? How would I leave a footprint on this planet to show my life had mattered? It quickly became clear to me that my purpose is in preparing the next generation to lead with love and to do so by loving them.

I founded College Moxie because of what my college experience meant to me. I recognized its significance more looking back than when I was actually in it. All of these amazing women believing the lie that they are not enough. I knew the feeling. I was one of them. It wasn't until after college that it all came together and hit me. I was lucky enough to have always known that I was loved by my parents and family. I also believed that God loved me, but I held on to deeply-rooted shame ingrained in my childhood culture that was hard for me to shake.

Separating what I knew of God's grace and mercy from what people of a particular church had taught me about God, was a challenging but necessary, and painstakingly slow task. Ironically, one of the most meaningful parts of my first conversation with my husband centered on betrayals we had both experienced in church communities, and having to come to terms with the fact that people will always fail us. So why was I often able to accept other people's shortcomings without finding room to have grace for my own? The answer was pride, fear, and shame.

Brene Brown beautifully states that guilt says, "I did a bad thing," whereas shame says, "*I* am bad." Guilt is the still small voice in our gut that knows we did something wrong and that we should apologize and try to fix it. But shame allows those mistakes to dissolve our self-worth, define us, and therefore limit us.

I distinctly remember a summer evening in my early 30's where I was crouched in a ball on the floor of my shower, sobbing yet again, over decisions made long ago that had brought about consequences in my relationships. I allowed this lying, negative voice in my head to convince me that anytime circumstances were disappointing, it was surely my fault, and my brain would point me to where I had previously stumbled, fallen, and failed. When positive things happened in my life, this voice told me that I wasn't worthy of them. This voice was manipulative, subtle, and soul-crushing. And because I wasn't calling it out, its influence grew.

But this time it ended differently. There on my shower floor, something shifted. In that moment of defeat and tearful remorse as I verbalized apologies for things long ago, I *felt* God say, "What are you talking about? I forgave you for that the first time you asked. I have washed it into the ocean and choose to remember it no more." I gasped as if the voice had been audible and started to process what this meant. If the perfect God of the Universe who created me in His image had forgiven me for everything that I continued to hold against myself- and even refused to return to it for leverage when it served a purpose- why in the world could *I* not let it go? Why was I making it so hard to love myself? It was the first time I realized my hypocrisy in acting as if my relationship with God could be earned, all while saying I believed otherwise. It hit me hard and took my breath. In that very moment, I realized something so powerful that I could never again look at my life, my dreams, my abilities, or my circumstances in the same way.

My freedom and empowerment came in this: There is nothing, *nothing* I- or you- can ever do to get outside of God's love. Not one. Single. Thing. My insistence that bad choices continued to define and limit me was actually a result of my pride. Voluntary, false sense-of-control-giving attachment to shame was completely limiting me and completely my choice. God loves me. God *is* love. And the time I was wasting reliving the ways I hadn't measured up to a standard of perfection given to me by an institution, not God- as if I really thought I was capable of living above my humanness- was truly arrogant and comical. I needed to let it go. As soon as I saw that and did it, my heart was filled with peace, and I was as free as Elsa in the ice castle. I now knew the power of something I could never un-know.

In our humanness, we will continue to fail, regardless of our commitment to growth and change. Sometimes bad decisions will leave us facing tough or lasting consequences. But that doesn't change the fact that there is nothing that we can ever do to cause Him to stop loving us. There is power in that love. There is *hope* in that love. And there is freedom in it, too. Freedom to give our all, expecting to stumble, but deciding *in advance* that we will learn from whatever results from our efforts, instead of allowing the results to define us and destroy our confidence. All that's left is vision, determination, and unbridled moxie.

Here is the biggest, toughest, most important thing that I have learned: forgiveness is hard but necessary. Whether forgiving ourselves or forgiving others, it is never easy to let something go. We see this "checks and balances" approach to worthiness as a way of controlling, comparing, and deciding that we are enough *only* when we are greater than someone else. We use this as a way to determine how we and others should rank in society, and when we should receive punishments or rewards. The problem is life is never fully fair and we never have all the facts.

Spinning our wheels to make strong judgments from behind a keyboard doesn't serve any of us. We want the right to judge because it gives us hope that we will be rewarded for what we do well, and that others will be held accountable for what they don't. I get it! It doesn't make sense by the world's standards to let bad behavior go when we, or those we care about, are wronged. *Injustice shouldn't happen.* No one should be wounded by the words or actions of others that cut so deeply that paralyzing effects can turn hearts to stone for the sake of self-preservation. It just shouldn't be.

The concepts of mercy and forgiveness are so counter to a culture that insists we act as judge and jury in all situations and with limited facts. But the truth is, we are better- we are *freed-* by choosing mercy and forgiveness. Nelson Mandela so perfectly said that "Resentment is like drinking poison and then hoping it will kill your enemies." Holding onto others' bad actions makes us feel like we are in control, but there is always a price to pay.

Unforgiveness eats at us in destructive, subtle ways. There is total freedom in forgiveness- not fairness- but freedom. When we can understand the depth of love that is given to us so freely, not contingent on our performance, then choosing to forgive becomes so much easier. And when we forgive ourselves in order to heal and grow, perhaps it becomes easier to forgive others, also. There is permission in forgiveness and motivation to chase our dreams fearlessly when we let the past go and decide to love ourselves fully. Think of the time we get back when we stop criticizing ourselves and replaying the narratives that focus on our imperfections! By the same token, knowing we are worthy of love as beautifully flawed humans, isn't it also easier to love others through their flaws? Let go of comparison. *Let go* of shame. Let go of expectations of perfection. Believe you are enough because you *are* enough. Wouldn't this shift make life so much more joyful?

We are all somewhere in a process of growth and nothing grows on mountaintops. We grow in the valleys of our most challenging circumstances, and every time we are there, we have a choice. Will we stay in a place of letting our wounds define us, or do we say, "This hurts, and although I'm having a hard time seeing past it, I will figure out what I can learn, give myself grace, do the work to heal as best I can, and I won't let it have been for nothing."

When we choose forgiveness, love will help heal us. When we choose to not be a hindrance to our purpose, then we get to make a difference every day. *No wasted pain.* Only added strength through experiences that result in tools to help us live a life that matters.

I spend my life encouraging women to know their worth and connect motives with behaviors to start choosing things that best serve them, rather than blindly accepting what has been normalized as necessary. I do this because it's what I *can* do.

It's where I am gifted; it's what I can control and it's what I wish I had been shown when I was their age. It is my purpose.

Oftentimes our purpose is rooted in our deepest struggles and most meaningful experiences. Have you determined yours and how they can be utilized for good? Is there something you're struggling to let go of that's in the way of you fully walking in your purpose? Where might you have more compassion and step back to realize that our legacy is in how we treat others and help propel them toward purpose or failure? Our words can lift others up or tear them down. Will we be crabs in a bucket of misery that loves company or will we root ourselves in goodness and find purpose in helping others achieve theirs, too?

Our world needs more love, and in every single thing we do, we have a choice in how we will lead and respond. *Choose love.* When we do, we discover that on the other side of that decision, there is freedom, self-acceptance, confidence, and the purest joy.

And there, in that place of gentle, calm, strength also lies what is unstoppable in you because *now*, you've found your Moxie.

Download your Workbook
Pages for Continuation here.

For a Desktop Experience, go to:
CollegeMoxie.org/how-to-find-your-moxie

College Moxie is a 501c3 nonprofit organization whose mission is to educate collegiate women on risks associated with campus life and empower them to know their worth so collectively we can raise the bar on campus culture. To support student scholarships and other current initiatives, please visit
CollegeMoxie.org/join-us

The Scott Carter Foundation is the result of Scott's dream to find a cure for children's cancers. After losing too many young friends to cancer, Scott asked to start an organization and utilize his sports collection to raise funds to find a cure. For more information on the foundation and how you can help, please visit
ScottCarterFoundation.org